Dog Obed

Training

Guide to Breaking Bad Habits and Preventing Them From Returning While Replacing Them With Positive Behavior to Turn Your Dog into a Great, Well-Behaved Pet Everyone Will Love

By Norman Thornton

Contents

Thank you for buying this book and I hope that you will find it useful. If you will want to share your thoughts on this book, you can do so by leaving a review on the Amazon page, it helps me out a lot.

Introduction

In case you have a dog, you are going to need to do more than simply feeding and providing toys. Almost every dog, regardless of the breed, is going to have certain bad behaviors and habits that you are going to need to break.

It is vital to make certain that you are sending out the appropriate message by removing any behavior that is considered improper and can ultimately result in embarrassment and shame.

There are various methods for handling every inappropriate behavior from the dog. Whatever you do, make certain that it works and that it's a thing that can make your dog change its way.

Because there are various behaviors for every event, you are going to discover that some of them are going to need special solutions. Obviously, you are going to need to consider your dog's breed. There are certain behaviors that originate from genes. So those are going to need to be handled appropriately.

Starting your dog on the proper foot initially is essential to getting them to comply with doing what you want. In case you wait up until later on, it might be hard for your dog and you to get things right.

It is essential to training your dog appropriately. Even if it's not your very first dog, you still have to undergo the procedure with each one you get. Make their environment an enjoyable one, and you will have a delighted dog.

You wish for your dog to be your best buddy and a member of your household. You wish for them to be that particular buddy when you have nobody else.

Here are certain things that you are going to read about within the following chapters:

- How To Prevent Biting

- How To Stop Barking and Howling .

- How To Stop Aggression.

You wish to have a pleased dog. Consequently, he is going to make you pleased. Dogs are distinct creatures. Once they get linked to you, they are linked, and there's no getting back.

Dogs are guy's best friend. They can supply things that no person can. A dog could be your shield from hurt, damage, and threat. They are going to quickly and easily come to your aid when they have to.

Nevertheless, they need to be trained correctly so as to do that. They need to do away with their bad habits to ensure they could be effective and reliable. As you are teaching them to do away with their bad habits, it is necessary that you have diligence. It is going to take some time for your dog to make those modifications that he has to make so as to be the dog that you desire.

Chapter 1: Biting

Although biting is looked at as a regular behavior, you ought to additionally remember that when dogs grow older, it might be a big threat to other people, and yourself.

It might be charming in the puppy phase, however as they get bigger, it's not adorable any longer. You need to begin when you still have a pup to get them to alter their habits concerning biting.

As a young puppy, biting is a learned behavior that originates from their mom. Due to the fact that they are not constantly with their mom, the person that looks after them needs to be in charge of that adjustment.

While still in the puppy phase, permit the puppy to have fun with other puppies. They like to engage with one another, and often, that is going to consist of biting. As they do this, they can discover how to manage themselves.

In case there's one puppy that is excessively aggressive, the others are going to go after the aggressive one for being too harsh. As they continue to have fun with one another, the puppy is going to find out how to control the biting.

You can begin really early as they're still a puppy when they are at least 4 to 6 weeks of age. Here are certain ideas that you can:

- Let the puppy understand that you feel pain as they bite you. You could be stern and state "no" or "ouch" to allow the puppy understand that it harmed you. The puppy is going to understand that they have actually gone too far, and they are going to consider what they have actually done.

- Gradually pull your hand away. Accomplishing this too quickly can lead to additional damage.

- In case they bite you once again, redo your spoken response. Step far from the puppy for some time. They are going to recognize that you do not value what they did and are going to determine that you do not wish to be around them.

- Provide a toy for chewing.

- Award the puppy when they are great and not biting.

- Be regular when you are teaching them to quit biting. Keep on letting the puppy understand that bites are not appropriate.

- Your puppy ought to go through an obedience class. This way, he can engage with other dogs as he grows older. He is going to find out about limitations with other dogs and people.

- As your puppy grows older and becomes a dog, he requires a great deal of exercise. Additionally, provide the dog with the possibility of playing outdoors so that he may get a bit of fresh air. Ensure he gets to play fetch and walk. This could assist them to not think about biting.

- Keep them on a routine with their exercises. They are going to get accustomed to doing things and are going to come to delight in that.

- Keep kids out of harm's reach by not leaving them with the pup alone. The pup might still be in the learning phase and might bite the kid.

- Avoid aggressive conduct with them. That can impact them to carry on biting.

- In case they carry on to bite regardless of your best shots, call your vet or a dog trainer for help.

Chapter 2: Whimpering, Howling And Severe Barking

There are times when whimpering, barking, and howling are typical for your dog. Nevertheless, in case you have a dog that continuously whimpers, barks, or howls, it can end up being an issue. It can end up being an issue for you, and it can additionally end up being an issue for your next-door neighbor in case you reside in an apartment or a neighborhood. You would get frequent complaints from them in case the issue is not fixed.

Here are several manners in which you can handle a dog that is continuously getting into trouble:

- Learn why the dog is whimpering, barking, or howling a lot. They might be starving, thirsty, or both. Ensure that the dog is constantly fed and constantly has water. Do not forget providing the dog with toys to ensure that they could remain occupied.

- Certain dogs do not like being on their own. They become disturbed when nobody is around, and it generates stress and anxiety. Along with being lonesome, they become stressed and start making all sorts of irritating sounds.

- Even in case you are at home, they have to discover how to be alone. Do not start constantly accommodating them when they whimper. In case you do, they are going to know that you will come each time. You'll have a tough time breaking that habit.

- In some cases, a dog is going to make sounds due to the fact that he has to utilize the restroom. You should take them after they eat, after an activity, after a snooze or when they are getting up. There are going to be other times, and when the dog gets trained, you are going to have the ability to figure everything out.

- After you have actually supplied food, toys, and water to the dog, they ought to be silent. Nevertheless, in case they are not, do not hesitate to let them understand that their conduct is not appropriate.

Chapter 3: Chewing

Chewing is common, beginning with young puppies all the way to a dog. Dogs believe that chewing is typical. Nevertheless, it is not always appropriate. In case you observe that your dog has issues with chewing, you are going to have to fix the issue as quickly as you discover it.

There are certain dogs that are going to chew anything that they are able to obtain. That consists of shoes, furnishings, and clothing. Naturally, these are things that you ought to keep away from them. It's not a great feeling to need to keep purchasing replacements.

Among the simplest remedies for this problem is getting your dog a range of toys that they can chomp on. Utilizing these toys could teach them what they may chew on and what is off limits. Plus, having a range of dog toys is going to keep them entertained.

Chewing on the toys is going to additionally keep their gums and teeth healthy. A few of the much better options for dog toys to chew on are ones that are flavored or scented. Regularly urge your dog to have fun with the toys.

As you are training them, additionally train them not to chew on things that there aren't meant to be chewing. It is additionally crucial that the location where the dog plays is kept clutter free. For your part, ensure that there are no clothes or other things that can prompt them to begin chewing.

In case the dog happens to obtain a thing that they're not meant to have, get their attention, and get rid of it. Then substitute it with a toy. Every time they do that, praise them for doing the appropriate thing. You can additionally stop them from chewing on your things by administering something that is going to make them step far from it, like Tabasco and other non-harmful things.

Chapter 4: Hopping On Others

Dogs love to hop on individuals. Nevertheless, there are certain dog owners who, in fact, urge this sort of conduct. They ought to remember that not everybody loves dogs and that their dog shouldn't hop up on everybody that they come across. Despite the fact that they are still adorable when they are young puppies, it can actually present an issue as they end up being mature dogs.

The issue with this is the fact that when the dogs grow older, they are heavier. The more the dogs weigh, the more hazardous hopping on individuals could be. Given that there are a great deal of individuals that do not like dogs, they are not going to appreciate one hopping on them and perhaps knocking them down.

In case it's a kid, it's even worse. The kid might be seriously hurt because of the weight of the dog. The dog owner might be in major trouble, regardless if it's their kid or not who got injured. Whether it's a grown-up or a kid, you might find yourself with a lawsuit in case you have not actually taught your dog to quit doing it.

The ideal time to teach him not to hop on other individuals is when he is young. It's simpler to teach them, and you will not have the hassle that you would in case the dog were older. As soon as you enable them to hop on other individuals, it could be tough to attempt to curb it as the dog ages. Their behavior is pretty much set and could be tough to break.

The way to perform this is that when they attempt to hop on somebody, you place their feet back on the ground in a mild and firm way. You can award and urge them as they keep on listening to you.

When you are urging your pet, you need to be at eye level. The dog is going to take you seriously when they discover that you are offering direct contact on their level. You can keep on bolstering this as long as you have to.

Ensure that everybody understands the rules and does not urge the dog to enable hopping on them. It could be puzzling when you have someone getting agitated and another person letting the dog to hop on them. The standard needs to be consistent, no matter who it is.

Chapter 5: Yanking And Tugging

Another behavioral issue that dogs have, beginning with their young puppy days, is yanking and tugging on a leash. This is another one that could be kicked off and urged by dog owners. Whenever you play games with the dog, like a tug of war, it makes the dogs believe that they can keep on doing the yank and tugging part. This can be a beginning a bad behavior that could be hard to break.

In case you have a body harness, it could be utilized when you are instructing your dog not to yank and tug. It can additionally be utilized when you need to re-train your dog to cease yanking and tugging. Work with the dog to ensure that they can accept and utilize the harness similarly as they would utilize a collar on their neck.

In case you are walking the dog, have a toy to ensure that you can make them remain by your side. You can additionally utilize a training collar. This collar could be utilized in case you are having issues teaching them not to yank and tug.

Even in case you utilize a choke chain, you can teach them similarly. Despite which one you utilize, make certain that it suits properly around their neck. It is crucial that it's not too large or too firm for them.

When you are walking your dog, the leash ought to stay loosened up. In case they yank ahead of you, modify directions to ensure that they are going to wind up behind you. This ought to be performed before it gets to the end of the leash. Do not let the dog or a young puppy yank you. As they are young, they have to get to know how to walk properly.

As they grow older and bigger, it's important that they are walking properly. As you are teaching him, do not pull or yank on their neck. Simply make a mild movement, and they are going to react. Utilizing excessive force can induce the dog to end up being upset.

Chapter 6: Improper Urination.

Improper urination for a dog owner could be extremely awkward. Not just that, mixed with defecation, it can create chaos. Prior to making adjustments, you need to get to the source of the issue. There might be various reasons why some dogs can not manage their bladders. As soon as you uncover the source of the issue, then you can carry on.

There are 2 kinds of improper urination, submissive and excitement. Both types will be explained.

Excitement Urination

When dogs get thrilled, they have a tendency to discharge control of their bladder and pee. It can occur when they get thrilled about noticing you. Although excitement urination is typical, it is not a lovely sight. It's a lot more awkward when you have somebody with you. For plenty of older dogs, it can actually present a huge issue.

Excitement urination generally begins when they are still a young pup. Considering that they are still little, they have a tendency not to manage their bladder. As a matter of fact, they might not understand what's taking place. What you do not wish to do is getting mad with them. That just makes it even worse for them you and them. They are going to keep on urinating since now you have actually disturbed them.

What you may do is incorporating prevention. You can stop him from becoming thrilled about particular things. Continuously subject him to a thing which is that is making him delighted and peeing. The more that you make it happen, the less fired up they are going to get, which, consequently, is going to stop the urination.

As they age and grow larger, they are going to have the ability to manage their bladder much more.

Submissive Urination

When it comes to submissive urination, this occurs amongst the group of dogs. The submissive dog lowers himself/herself and begins to pee. The other dogs notice what the leader is doing, and after that, they do the same.

When dogs display this sort of behavior, they are typically insecure. Dogs of this kind have actually formerly been abused by somebody else.

Dogs who demonstrate submissive urination are normally revealing their insecurity. Unsocialized and formerly mistreated dogs typically show submissive urination. These dogs have to be shown that there are better-suited methods to demonstrate their submissive standing, like licking the owner's hand or shaking hands.

You can additionally disregard the urination, however, ensure that you tidy up the mess. You could additionally instruct the dog to raise their paw, command them to take a seat, together with additional obedience commands. Accomplishing this is going to get the dog's respect.

It is not a simple job to handle urination problems; nevertheless, you still have to be consistent. When they are progressing, you ought to award them constantly.

Do not penalize the dog for unsuitable urination since it is going to just make the circumstances worse for you both.

Chapter 7: Not Heeding Your Call.

It is necessary for dog owners to understand how crucial it is for their dog to get to them when called. When they fall short of heeding the owner's call, it may spell trouble. In case the dog is engaged and does not arrive when called, they can bump into traffic and get struck by a vehicle.

Regrettably, there are some negligent owners who permit their dog to go totally free without a leash. This is not a great idea. The owner ought to constantly have the dog on a leash. As a matter of fact, numerous metropolitan locations demand that a dog is on a leash, or the owner might deal with fines. Once they can wander unattended and free, the dog couldn't care less about complying with the owner's orders.

When the dog has this understanding, they are going to postpone heeding the owner's calls, if they come whatsoever. In case you have actually not enabled this kind of behavior to occur, do not start it. Nevertheless, in case you have, do your finest to reverse the circumstance. You need to train them to react when you state "come here" and other commands. This remains in the very best interest of people and other animals.

When you utilize the "come here" command, utilize it in a manner that is going to be helpful for the dog. Have fun with him initially, and after that, do other things with him. In case you utilize the command, and after that, clean him up later, that is not going to be harmful. Ensure that the dog does not link the command with a negative experience.

Your dog is going to constantly remain in the learning phase. It is necessary that each procedure of training and teaching is a thing that is positive. This way, they will not be reluctant to do whatever it is that you desire them to do.

Every time you order the dog to come, offer him a prize. It does not need to be fancy. Motivating the dog can consist of patting them on the head or scratching behind their ears. You can additionally offer them dog snacks if you choose so. Just as long as it's a thing which makes them feel excellent. As you carry this out, you need to be consistent.

Chapter 8: Chasing After Individuals And Things

Dogs are recognized to run after moving items. A prime instance is a mailman bringing the mail. They are typical targets for dogs. Another thing that dogs run are wheels on a vehicle as the vehicle is moving. Nevertheless, this is not appropriate, and it could be harmful to the dog along with the target they are going after.

You need to train your dog not to go after individuals and things. The quicker you begin, the much better the likelihood you have of getting the dog to comply with you. The ideal time to begin is when the dog is still little and not intimidating.

It's a lot more essential for those types that are big and those that are recognized to have bold tendencies. When individuals are gone after by a dog, they are afraid and begin to run. They do not recognize what that dog is going to do.

Depending upon the type, some are simpler to train not to go after individuals or things. Those that are utilized for hunting or herding functions are most likely to keep on chasing. It is not an excellent idea to allow a dog to run totally free in case they have actually not been taught not to go after people and things. Even if they have been taught, they still have to stay on a leash when outside.

Whenever you are teaching your dog, do it in a secure location that is built-in. A perfect location would be a fenced backyard. By doing this, the dog is going to have the ability to focus on what you are attempting to do with him. You want the dog to comprehend that you are attempting to teach him the appropriate ways. Additionally, the dog needs to be provided with a possibility to go over the habits that you are attempting to teach him.

You ought to additionally train the dog in your house. This is additional manner of keeping the dog in a regulated environment. Put a leash on the dog. You and the dog are going to stand at one end of the room or a hallway. Get a little ball and wave it before the dog.

You are not going to allow the dog to touch the ball. Roll the ball to the other end and utilize the command "off." This command allows the dogs to recognize that they are not to chase the ball. Nevertheless, in case they begin to pursue it, state the command "off" once again and carefully and strongly yank the leash.

It is vital that the dog does not touch the ball whatsoever. In case you enable him to perform so, then they are going to believe that the command "off" implies that they can touch it. Do this a couple of times or up until the dog has actually discovered what the command implies. After the dog has actually gotten the message, provide him with a snack as a prize for getting to know that command.

Attempt the identical thing, however, go to another area. Redo the procedure once again in more rooms of your house. After you think that your dog has actually learned what he has to know, you may do it without having the leash. Bear in mind that you need to stay in a regulated location. It might take a while for your dog to master this. Be persistent up until you are positive that he has actually broken the habit of chasing.

Perform a test to check if your dog has really learned from your instruction. Get somebody to function as a jogger or a walker. The dog must not see them. As a matter of fact, the individual that you pick ought to be a complete stranger to the dog.

Have the dog on the leash and permit the individual to jog or jog numerous times. Throughout this time, you are going to use the "off" command. See if the dog is going to stay still or attempt to chase the individual. If they attempt to run, carefully and securely yank on the leash. In case they sit tight, you can provide a reward.

Chapter 9: Escaping And Wandering.

You must never ever permit your dog to leave your house and wander in the neighborhood. That is careless on your part. It can additionally present a risk to your dog and the locals in the location. In many locations, you have to have the dog on a leash. If you let this take place, you might get in trouble and most likely deal with a fine.

There are occasions when it's not your fault that the dog has actually gone astray. Some dogs are going to work out an escape strategy on their own. Once they go out, they are going to pursue anything in sight. That consists of people, vehicles, or anything that makes a motion. Working to stop this from occurring is simpler than attempting to get your dog back when they have actually gone out.

Among the important things that you may do is getting rid of everything that is going to prompt your dog to escape. You need to keep your dog occupied. In case they are bored, they are going to wish to escape, and they are going to plan to do it.

In case they have lots of toys, together with sleeping arrangements and water, they will not consider escaping. They are going to be too occupied getting their rest and playing.

In case you have a dog who has a great deal of energy, they are going to wish to leave. They are not utilizing their energy, and it makes them uneasy and want to go out. Enable the dog to work off the energy that has actually accumulated within them. They are going to feel much better later on.

You need to additionally design your home to ensure that it will not be simple for your dog to escape. Ensure that the fencing is good enough that they are going to remain in a regulated environment. In case you have a dog who has a routine of digging, you might need to put metal stakes in the soil.

You might additionally need to make the fence taller in case your dog has a tendency of hopping. The final option is to keep your dog constrained when nobody is at home to monitor him.

It is essential that you do whatever you have to do to prevent your dog from leaving and wandering around. They could be a risk to others and to themselves too. There are individuals out there who don't mind getting their hands on a dog who is not theirs. So it's essential that you take suitable actions to make sure your dog and other people are safe.

Chapter 10: Fighting

It is essential that your dog is maintained under control in case they come across another dog. Your dog might not be a provocateur when it concerns fighting, however, the other dog might be. Make certain that you have actually taught your dog to obey. They ought to have the ability to comply with every one of your orders.

Here are some manners in which you can stop your dog from fighting:

- Ensure that the dog's collar is fitting appropriately. It must not be too firm or loose.

- Bring a spray bottle and an umbrella for security.

- In case an aggressive dog shows up, order your dog to sit and look elsewhere. Have your umbrella handy.

- Neither you nor your dog must run. This simply intensifies the circumstance.

- Place the umbrella in between the dogs to ensure that it opens.

- Place your foot ahead and state, "Stop!" and after that, open the umbrella.

- When you open the umbrella, the aggressive dog is going to attempt to leave.

- In case you utilize the spray bottle, aim for the instigator's nose and state "Stop!" and spray. Attempt to stay clear of the eyes.

- So long as your dog is taught effectively, they are going to do what you say.

- In case the spray bottle or umbrella technique does not do the job, you and your dog pull back gradually.

- Stay clear of eye contact with the instigator. It simply makes him more susceptible to attacking, whether it's your dog or you.

- In case the other dog is incredibly aggressive, they might still attempt to attack. You might need to look for extra assistance.

Chapter 11: Begging

Certain dogs have a behavior of begging. This is a simple habit to break. You need to be consistent when you are attempting to break the habit. In case there are other individuals in your home, they need to do be consistent too.

- Obtain a thing that your dog does not like. You can have a go at fruits like grapes that are bitter. You may obtain these from pet shops. Likewise, attempt utilizing Tabasco sauce mixed with vinegar.

- Provide your dog with sampling to discover whether he likes it. Utilize other foods that you believe the dog might not eat. In case they do not eat what you give them, they dislike the flavor or the odor of the food.

- As you feed the dog, offer him the food which he does not want to smell or eat. In case the dog begins to beg, offer him a bit of food in addition to the things that he does not want.

- The dog is going to recognize the taste and will not wish to eat it. In case there are other individuals who are eating, have them help you with this test.

- Be consistent and utilize a thing that your dog does not like. The more consistent you remain, the more the dog is going to get the hint.

- You can additionally state "no" regularly. Make certain that you mean it, or else, your dog is going to understand that you do not mean it.

Ultimately, your dog is going to get the hint and quit begging. However, it is necessary that you feed him routine meals to ensure that he will not become hungry and begin begging.

Chapter 12: Keeping The Dog Out Of The Trash

Dogs are drawn to trash. They love how it smells and believe that they could discover some leftovers that they can consume. In some cases, they just want to search through garbage to deal with their feeling of boredom. You can break this habit. Here are some manners in which you may do that:

- In case you see them going through the trash, you may walk up on them. Call them out by letting them know that they are being bad and that they have to leave the garbage.

- Enforce discipline on your dog. Place them in a room and allow them to have a long time alone. Tell them why they are by themselves in the room.

- Repeat the process to bolster your stance on your dog not entering the trash. Ultimately, through your steadfastness and consistency, they are going to learn to stop doing that.

- Make certain that you are performing your part by shutting out every chance for your dog to enter the trash.

- Change the garbage. In case you do not have a trash bin that has a cover that just works with your foot, you ought to obtain one. Ensure that your trash bin remains closed.

- In case you have garbage to be thrown away, do it immediately. Letting it lie around is going to just entice your dog to search through more garbage.

- Do not be vigorous when attempting to get your dog to quit digging through your garbage. Be persistent with him.

- A mild, yet firm reaction is going to resonate with your dog rather than a vigorous one.

- Provided that you are regularly making an effort, your dog is going to ultimately get the hint.

Chapter 13: Aggressive Conduct

You might have a dog who is aggressive in their conduct. This could be a daunting circumstance since you do not understand when they wish to attack. So as to blow off some steam, you may take him to the park. Nevertheless, attempt to keep him far from other dogs to protect against an attack on other people or dogs.

- Make sure that the dog has his focus on you to ensure that he could be distracted from noticing other dogs.

- In case another dog is coming close, yank the leash sideways.

- In case you pull the leash directly, you are offering your dog control. Maintaining the leash sideways guarantees that your dog is going to have less control.

- In case you feel your dog beginning to act out, attempt to divert him by creating sounds that he would react to. Nevertheless, do not shout or scream.

- Keep your dog far from other dogs. When you notice that he is beginning to alter his habits, provide him with a reward.

- Get together with another dog to ensure that they are able to meet. Maintain your dog on the leash. Discover a location which your dog is not acquainted with. Your dog is going to end up being territorial in a familiar location and feel endangered by another dog.

- Observe how your dog responds when meeting a different dog. In case you see that he's not too happy, then proceed. A few of the indications are stiffening, growling, or drawing on the leash to get nearer to the other dog. It's much more effective to be proactive instead of being reactive.

- See whether you can discover other dogs that you want to connect with your dog and redo this procedure until you are pleased with the results.

- In case your dog continues to have aggressive propensities, enroll him in a dog obedience class. There are certified dog instructors that can deal with your dog in a group. A great deal of times, a group environment could be much better therapy for a dog.

Here are a few other things to observe about your aggressive dog:

- Think about neutering your dog in case it's a male dog. After that, they will not feel as dominant or have such aggressive tendencies.

- Aggressive dogs must not be penalized in a physical way. That just intensifies the issue.

- Utilize a leash that can be retracted. It can aid when you are meeting other dogs. Your dog is not going to feel confined, and you may continue to manage his motions.

- Even if your dog wags its tail, that does not indicate that they have an interest in getting along with the other dogs.

It is necessary that you continue to regularly keep control over things, no matter whether you are at home, at the park, or any place where you meet other dogs.

Chapter 14: Digging Up Holes

Walking in your backyard, you might discover a great deal of holes. In case your dog hangs back there, you do not need to guess where they originated from. Ultimately, sooner rather than later, you are going to have to train your dog how to cease digging up holes in your backyard.

Not just is it unattractive, you are going to additionally need to come out of your pocket to get your backyard fixed. Plus, in case you accomplish it yourself, that is time devoted there while you might have been doing anything else.

Dogs aren't thinking as they are carrying this out. They might get bored of having fun with the toys, and they are not necessarily hungry. Something that you must not do is using punishment to get them to quit.

In case you do attempt to penalize them, you might deal with the dog rebelling. You are going to have to discover the source of why they are digging, to start with. Then you are going to have the ability to go from there to change things.

Here are several things that you can have a go at to get your dog to quit digging holes in your backyard:

- Put barriers in particular parts of your backyard to keep the dog out. They ought to be put in the parts where he usually digs holes. Once they understand that their preferred spots are obstructed, they are going to quit attempting to dig additional holes.

- You might wish to have a sprinkler that is going to sprinkle water on your dog. Dogs are not very eager about having water splashed on them.

- Make certain that your dog gets a lot of physical activity. That can assist them to quit thinking about wishing to dig holes in your backyard. Among the primary reasons why they do it is due to the fact they become bored and believe that they have absolutely nothing else they can do.

- Make time to have fun with your dog. When they understand that you are spending time with them, they are going to be less probable to consider damaging your backyard.

- Your dog ought to have a lot of toys to keep them occupied. Make certain that they have a wide array to ensure that they will not get tired quickly.

- If having fun with them and taking them out for routine exercise is insufficient, you might wish to buy a sandbox. Or you can segment off a part of your backyard where they are permitted to dig. You can additionally permit them to have treats and toys in that part. Once they get used to it, they are not going to see the requirement to dig holes anyplace else in your backyard.

- Dogs do not enjoy the heat, so they are going to dig holes and utilize the dirt to maintain them cool. If you wish to dissuade them from digging, provide a location with shade and supply them with a lot of water.

- One thing that you may do to keep your dog from digging might not be an enjoyable one. Nevertheless, you might be amazed to discover that it could be helpful. You can put a bit of waste in the holes which are being dug up. As soon as the dog reaches the waste, they are going to wish to quit digging in your backyard.

Chapter 15: OCD

Obsessive-Compulsive Disorder (OCD) is when individuals do things repeatedly, and they do not understand why. It is odd conduct, and there are many individuals who struggle with it. Nevertheless, did you ever consider that dogs could struggle with OCD as well?

Dogs acquire OCD when they are struggling with boredom or stress. They can additionally experience it when they are handling anxiety. For a dog owner, handling OCD could be a pain in the neck. They can't instantly determine why their dog is acting in such a manner.

Dogs can act out in a range of ways, consisting of harming things, ruining backyards, being aggressive towards others, and barking. As soon as these end up being recurring, the dog has actually become part of the world of OCD.

In case you notice that your dog is bored, you are going to need to discover extra activities for them to do. Or you are going to have to devote more time to doing activities with them that they like.

Dogs love it when you spend good quality time with them. They resemble kids; in case you do not hang out with them, they are going to enter into things that they shouldn't entering into.

Your dog might sense that they are not obtaining adequate exercise. Spend more time having fun with them. Your dog might sense that you are not engaging with them sufficiently. Because they can't talk, the only manner in which they can demonstrate their aggravation is to redo certain actions up until you see it.

In case your dog is stressed out, speak with your vet. As soon as your dog gets in that mode, he can end up being aggressive and place others at risk, consisting of the dog himself. Your vet can offer your dog the meds to soothe him.

Depending upon what sort of breed you are dealing with, they might be genetically predisposed to OCD. There are particular ones, like German Shepherds and English Bull Terriers, that are recognized to connect OCD to their hereditary history.

Whatever it may be, as soon as you learn your dog has OCD, it is essential to get the assistance right away to ensure that they can live a regular life.

Conclusion

You can assist your dog in transforming their bad habits by regularly working with them. Consistency is crucial in order for your pet to make the adjustment that you wish to see. Stay with your guidelines and do not enable anybody else that gets in contact with the dog to do things differently.

As soon as your techniques and training are carved in stone, your dog is going to begin to get accustomed to them, and ultimately, is going to do away with the bad habits. You are going to have a challenging time with a dog that does not wish to comply with your orders and declines to conform.

You are going to be less stressed out as soon as your dog is at ease and is following your orders. It is necessary that they do that. You are going to feel good about taking them out and letting them be on the move.

Dogs resemble kids-- you need to keep supporting them and supplying them with love and assistance. Simultaneously, they need to understand that they need to accept correction so as to be an effective member of your household.

I hope that you enjoyed reading through this book and that you have found it useful. If you want to share your thoughts on this book, you can do so by leaving a review on the Amazon page. Have a great rest of the day.

Printed in Great Britain
by Amazon

26873285R00037